Acknowledgement of Land & of the Traditional Owners of this Land

I would like to acknowledge the Gadigal people of the Eora Nation, upon whose stolen land I stand on today.
I recognise that this land was never terra nullius — the land belonging to these peoples was never ceded, given up, bought or sold.
I would like to pay my respects to Aboriginal Elders past, present and emerging, and I extend this acknowledgement to all Aboriginal and Torres Strait Islander people.

"Are you an OUTSIDER?"

CONTENTS

1: I Like to Offend
(Mi Piace Offendere)
2: Savage River
(Fiume Selvaggio)
3: I Was Born Under a "Good" Sign
(Sono Nato Sotto Un Segno "Buono")
4: Salvation
(Salvezza)
5: LO♥E Has DIED
(L'Amore è Morto)
6: The Promised Land
(La Terra Promessa)
7: Useless & Pointless Knowledge
(Conoscenza Inutile e Inutile)
8: Will You Be Ready to Die?
(Sarai Pronto a Morire?)
9: The Pain of Birth
(Il Dolore Della Nascita)
10: A Good Life, Well Lived
(Una Bella Vita, Ben Vissuta)
11: Tread Gently
(Procedi Delicatamente)
12: Oh my GOD, I'm Here All Alone!
(Oh Mio Dio, Sono Qui Tutto Solo!)
13: Fatal Attraction
(Attrazione Fatale)
14: Pleasure Machine
(Macchina del Piacere)
15: Black Sheep
(Pecora Nera)
16: The Child that Never Grew Up
(Il Bambino Che Non è Mai Cresciuto)
17: I've Gotta Get My Fun
(Devo Divertirmi)

CONTENTS

18: Deaf, Dumb & Blind
(Sordi, Muti e Ciechi)
19: Will You Let Me LO♥E You?
(Mi Permetterai di Amarti?)
20: I Never Really Was Impressed
(Non Sono Mai Stato Davvero Colpito)
21: State of Flux
(Stato di Flusso)
22: I've Got a Dirty Mind
(Ho Una Mente Sporca)
23: Gemini Dream
(Sogno dei Gemelli)
24: I Am Not a Predator
(Non Sono Un Predatore)
25: A "Moment" Lasts Forever
(Un "Attimo" Dura per Sempre)
26: The Universe is Always Talking
(L'Universo Parla Sempre)
27: Sexless Women
(Donne Senza Sesso)
28: The Girl from Ipanema & Einstein
(La Ragazza di Ipanema e Einstein)
29: Let Me Entertain You
(Lascia che ti Intrattenere)
30: My Life as a Wog: Haggling
(La Mia Vita da Wog: Mercanteggiare)
31: Don't FUCKING Work at All!
(Non Lavorare Affatto, CAZZO!)
31: My Hands
(Le Mie Mani)
32: Torn Between Fucks
(Diviso Tra Una Scopata e L'altra)

CONTENTS

33: And the World Took Him to His Grave
(E Il Mondo Lo Portò Nella Sua Tomba)
34: Sleeping Isn't Death!
(Dormire Non è la Morte!)
35: When the Sky Falls Down
(Quando il Cielo Cade)
36: Predator
(Predatore)
37: Self-Control
(Autocontrollo)
38: People Can Change
(Le Persone Possono Cambiare)
39: Boring
(Noioso)
40: None of Us Are Real
(Nessuno di Noi è Reale)
41: Don't Ask Me for Any Advice
(Non Shiedermi Nessun Consiglio)
42: Fool's Hope
(La Speranza dello Sciocco)
43: Alchemy
(Alchimia)
44: Lonesome Highway
(Autostrada Solitaria)
45: "Personable" Shit
(Merda "personale")
46: Pissing in the Wind
(Pisciare nel vento)
47: Control
(Controllo)
48: Charlatan
(Ciarlatano)
49: The Game of Life
(Il Gioco della Vita)
50: Out of the NOISE
(Fuori dal RUMORE)

I Like to Offend

(Mi Piace Offendere)

I like to be *controversial*.
I like to *polarise*.
I like to be *loud*.
I like to *SHOUT*.
I like to *talk*...
...*A LOT!*

I like to put *"people off"*.
I like to create *contradictions*.
I like to *ridicule*.
I like to *argue*.
I like to be *rude*.
I like to be *crude*.
I like to be *obnoxious*.
I like to be *"bombastic"*.
I like to be a *"smart-alec"*.
I like to *fart in public*...
...*and blame you!*
I like to *swear*.
I like to say words such as...
...*VAGINA*.
...*PUSSY*.
...*COCK*.
...*PRICK*.
...*SHIT*.
...*SHITHOLE*
...*ARESHOLE*.
...*FUCK*.

I'm a *"Cosmic Shit-stirrer"*!
Because...
...*I like to OFFEND!*

"The Don"
20.10.2023

Savage River

(Fiume Selvaggio)

It ain't no bubbling brook.
It ain't no tributary.
It ain't the Mississippi River.
No *"peaceful waters"* on this river.
No dam gonna stop it from flowing.
Even GOD is scared of it!

It is treacherous.
Full of rapids and waterfalls.
With unforeseen dangers at every bend.
It is not for the weak of mind.
Or those with *"super human"* strength.
It will NOT be enough.
Do not even attempt to ride her or try to tame her.
You WILL fail.
It will claim you...
...as it has claimed many others before you.

Foolish souls!
You will FAIL!
It will KILL you!
You will DIE!

That is the fate of anyone to conquer...
...the Savage River.
It is as though Nature herself is talking directly to us through her and saying...
..."Leave me alone and let me be!"
"I am Savage River and you cannot tame me"...
..."For I MUST be FREE!"

"The Don"
22.10 2023

I Was Born Under a "Good" Sign

(Sono Nato Sotto Un Segno "Buono")

I was born under a *"good"* sign.
I was *lucky*!
It was born under the sign of the *"Fish"*.
Yes...
...*"Pisces"*!
With *"Capricorn"* ascending...
....and *"Sagittarius"* descending.
I'm a *"water"* being.
Very *"fluidic"*.
Very *"sensitive"*.
Very *"creative"*.
I don't know about that one I'm sure of...
...is that I'm FORTUNATE!

So that's got to be a *"good" thing*.
Because...
...I'm born under a "good" sign.

"The Don"
22.10.203

Salvation

(Salvezza)

Don't bother *looking for it.*
Don't bother *seeking it.*
Don't bother *expecting it.*
Don't bother *pursuing it.*
Don't bother trying to possess it.
Don't bother *praying for it.*
Don't bother to *DIE for it.*
Don't bother to *believe it is HEAVEN.*

Don't try to *erase your past.*
Don't try to *deny your actions.*
Don't try to *excuse your behaviour.*
Don't try to *hide who you REALLY are!*

You CAN'T!

Don't try to *buy it.*
Don't try to *lie for it.*
Don't try to *steal it.*
Don't try to *go to HELL for!*

You CAN'T!

Because...
...it's a MYTH!
It doesn't *EXIST!*
There is NO salvation!

There ain't NO...
...SALVATION!
No, no, no!

There ain't NO...
...SALVATION!
Do you hear me?

There ain't NO...
...SALVATION!
NO...
...SALVATION!

"The Don"
25.10.2023

LO♥E Has DIED

(L'Amore è Morto)

The battle is over.
The war has been won.
We have lost!
We have been DEFEATED!
To the *"victor"* go the spoils.

LO♥E has *lost!*
LO♥E has been *defeated*.
LO♥E has been *destroyed*.
LO♥E has been KILLED.
LO♥E has DIED!

EVIL has *WON*!
EVIL has *triumphed*!
EVIL has *taken over*.
EVIL is *CONTROL*!

Now is the time to cry!
Because...
...*LO♥E has DIED*!

"The Don"
27.10.2023

The Promised Land
(La Terra Promessa)

We are living on it...
...Planet Earth *(Tera, Ghia)* call her whatever you will.
Our *"Mother"*.
This is the *"Promised Land"*!

"The Don"
27.10.2023

Useless & Pointless Knowledge

(Conoscenza Inutile e Inutile)

What ya gonna do with it?
It's NOT going to help you!
In fact...
...it's gonna FUCK you up!

Get rid of this useless & pointless knowledge.

Get rid of YOUR useless & pointless knowledge.

"The Don"
27.10.2023

Will You Be Ready to Die?

(Sarai Pronto a Morire?)

Will you be ready to die?
When the times comes.
And WILL come!
You can't run AWAY from it!
Will you be ready?
Will you be ready to die?

Have you got ALL your affairs in order?
I'm not talking about MATERIAL ones...
...NO!
I'm talking about your *SPIRITUAL* ones...
...those that REALLY matter!
When the time comes...
...the time to DIE!
Will you be ready to die?

"The Don"
28.10.2023

THE PAIN OF BIRTH
(Il Dolore Della Nascita)

WOW!
What a POWERFUL statement!
And what is the pain that it is referring to?
Maybe, it's the realisation of the world we have been born into!
Or...
...maybe, it's the knowledge that we will DIE!
Maybe...
...it's BOTH!

"Ahhhhhhhhhhhhhhhhhhhh!"

"The Don"
28.10.2023

A Good Life, Well Lived
(Una Bella Vita, Ben Vissuta)

Can you agree with that?
Is your life...
...a life well lived?

"The Don"
28.10.2023

TREAD GENTLY

(Procedi Delicatamente)

Tread gently & softly.
Leave as small a footprint as possible.
Try to cause as little damage as you possibly can as you stumble forward through life.

"The Don"
30.10.2023

Oh my GOD, I'm Here All Alone!

(Oh Mio Dio, Sono Qui Tutto Solo!)

"Oh my GOD...
...am I here ALL ALONE?"

"Oh my
...I'm here ALL ALONE!"

"Oh my GOD...
...I'm here ALL ALONE?

AHHHHHHHHHHHHHHHHHHH!

"You walk into the room with your pencil in your hand
You see somebody naked and you say, "Who is that man?"
You try so hard but you don't understand
Just what you will say when you get home
Because something is happening here but you don't know what it is
Do you, Mr. Jones?

You raise up your head and you ask, "Is this where it is?"
And somebody points to you and says, "It's his"
And you say, "What's mine?" and somebody else says, "Well, what is?"
And you say, "Oh my God, am I here all alone?"
But something is happening and you don't know what it is
Do you, Mr. Jones?

You hand in your ticket and you go watch the geek
Who immediately walks up to you when he hears you speak
And says, "How does it feel to be such a freak?"
And you say, "Impossible!" as he hands you a bone
And something is happening here but you don't know what it is
Do you, Mr. Jones?"

"Ballad of a Thin Man"
Songwriter: Bob Dylan

"The Don"
30.10.2023

Fatal Attraction

(Attrazione Fatale)

Attraction...
...what's that ALL about?
How does exist?
If so...
...how does it work?
Well...
...I believe it was Isaac Newtown (a very noted physicist) that came up with a law...
..."The Law of Attraction".

It was a very simple law.
In fact, quite an obvious one really.
It started that...
..."Opposites attract"!
Which seems to be plausible enough.

But it is that necessarily true?
Is attraction just physical?
Or is there more to it?

Well...
...I know that there are different sorts of attraction.

There's...
...sexual attraction,
There's...
...intellectual attraction,
There's...
...spiritual attraction,
There's...
...."Fatale" attraction.
There's...
...unwanted attraction
There's...
...blind attraction.

Some confuse attraction with LO E
Don't YOU do that!

Maybe it's just a chemical thing that affects your brain...
...your emotions,
...your desires,
...your fantasies,
...your passions.

All I know though, is that...
...attraction, whatever it is,
...is mysterious!

Make sure you don't fall for *"Fatal Attraction"!*

"The Don"
31.10.2023

Pleasure Machine

(Macchina del Piacere)

You might be a *"Pleasure machine"*.
But...
...*you're NOT romantic!*

"The Don"
01.11.2023

Black Sheep

(Pecora Nera)

Are you...
...different?
Are you...
...unusual?
Are you...
...a loner?
Are you...
...a rebel?
Are you...
...a non-conformist?
Are you...
...always an outsider?
Are you...
...a "Black sheep"?

Do you find that you...
...don't fit in?
...don't belong?
...people don't understand you?
Feel like a square peg in a round hole.
Well maybe...
...you are a "Black sheep".

Do people make you feel like there's something wrong with you?
Well I hate to tell you...
...but
...you are a "Black sheep"!

I know I am!

*"Well...
...I'm BLAAAACK!
BLAAAACK!
BLAAAACK!
Well I'm Back in Black!
Back in Black!"*

*BLAAAACK!
BLAAAACK!
BLAAAACK!
Well I'm Back in Black!
Back in Black!"*

"Back In Black"- AC/DC

"The Don"
03.11.2023

The Child that Never Grew Up

(Il Bambino Che Non è Mai Cresciuto)

That's me!
In my mind I'm still 14.
Not an old man of 64.

In my mind I'm still a child.
I act like a child.
I behave like a child.
I think like a child.
I feel like a child.
That's because...
...I'm the child that never grew up.

People tell me all the time to...
..."grow up".
..."act my age"
...be "mature".
...be "sensible".
..."shut the FUCK up".
I can't help it.
Because...
...I'm the child that never grew up.

I'm TOO talkative (I talk a lot)!
I'm TOO loud.
I'm TOO sarcastic.
I'm TOO obnoxious.
I'm TOO crazy.
I'm TOO flippant.
I'm TOO dismissive.
I'm TOO RUDE!
I'm TOO CRUDE!
That's because...
...I'm the child that never grew up.

I NEVER shut up.
I NEVER take things seriously
I NEVER stop taking the micky.
I NEVER stop making fun of things.
I NEVER stop ridiculing.
I NEVER stop harassing people.
I NEVER stop having FUN!
I NEVER stop making JOKES.
And that's because...
...I'm the child that never grew up!

"For God's sake grow the FUCK up & STOP like a CHILD!"

"But I AM a child, trapped in an old man's body!"

"The Don"
04.11.2023

I've Gotta Get My Fun

(Devo Divertirmi)

What is your fun?
Is it watching sport on the TV?
Or is it...
...reading a good book?
Maybe it's binging on the latest Netflix sensation?
Maybe is its soulful music that tears your heart apart.
Or maybe it's words that is your fun.
Words are your *"plaything"*...
...your domain.
...your world!

Maybe your fun is more of the *"BODY"*?
...more "CORPOREAL"?
...more SALACIOUS?
Maybe you're a *"Player"*?
...you like to have fun in the nude?
...with someone else...
...also naked?
Maybe your fun is having blissful, unbridled SEX?
...FUCKING!
As much as YOU can GET!
Any time of day...
...or night.
Having sex is you fun.

Whatever your fun is...
...it's OK by me.

But...
...let me have MY fun!

So, we can ALL have fun!

Enjoy!

"The Don"
08.11.2023

Deaf, Dumb & Blind

(Sordi, Muti e Ciechi)

Hear nothing!
Say nothing!
See nothing!
That's how we survive in this world!

We are...
...*deaf*...
...*dumb and*...,
...*blind*!

"The Don"
08.11.2023

Will You Let Me LO♥E You?
(Mi Permetterai di Amarti?)

Will you let me LO♥E you?
Of course, I'll let you LO♥E me!
And I'll try to LO♥E you, just as much back.

"The Don"
08.11.2023

I Never Really Was Impressed
(Non Sono Mai Stato Davvero Colpito)

"With objects & material things...
...well...
...I never really was impressed."

-"Tangled Up In Blue" The New York Version
- Bob Dylan

"The Don"
09.11.2023

State of Flux

(Stato di Flusso)

State of *commotion*.
State of *confusion*.
State of *chaos*.
State of *disorder*.
State of *anarchy*.
State of *hatred*.
State of *cruelty*.
State of *terror*.
State of *horror*.
State of *destruction*.
State of *annihilation*.
State of *violence*.
State of *war*.

We're living in a *"State of flux"*!

"The Don"
14.11.2023

I've Got a Dirty Mind

(Ho Una Mente Sporca)

You have *"wicked"* look in your eyes.
A look that tells me that there's *"more"* to you than meets the eye.
With those *"kiss my lips"*, lips!
With...
...that "come hither look".
...that "look" that is inviting.
...that "look" that is enticing.
...that "look" that is alluring.
...that "look" that speaks "sex".
...that "look" that says "I am very FUCKABLE".
...that "look" that says, "I have a dirty mind".

Do you?
Do you have a *"dirty mind"*?

"Yes"...
...*"I have a "dirty mind!"*

Why not put our two "dirty" minds together and make some dirt?
"Ok!"

WOW...
...I can't wait until our two minds merge!

When our two *"dirty minds"* become one!

"The Don"
18.11.2023

Gemini Dream

(Sogno dei Gemelli)

A *"Gemini Dream"* is when two people have the same dream...
...at the same time!

What is it called when ALL people have the same dream...
...at the same time?

"The Don"
23.11.2023

I Am Not a Predator

(Non Sono Un Predatore)

I am not a predator...
...just because I'm male!

"The Don"
24.11.2033

A "Moment" Lasts Forever

(Un "Attimo" Dura per Sempre)

A *"Moment"* lasts forever.
It is timeless!
It is without bounds...
...without limits.

It only dies when you come back...
...to...
...*"REALITY"*!

"The Don"
25.11.2023

Sexless Women

(Donne Senza Sesso)

It seems that after about fifty-five years old *(or thereabouts)...*
...a woman becomes SEXLESS!
...that's right!
They don't want sex anymore!
They seem completely disinterested.

It has become a *burden.*
It has become an *obligation.*
It has become an *abhorrence*!

What's your experience?

"The Don"
03.12.2023

The Girl from Ipanema & Einstein
(La Ragazza di Ipanema e Einstein)

Did you know that Einstein went to Brazil...
...Ipanema in fact.
And there on Ipanema Beach he met the *"Girl from Ipanema"*.

What did they talk about?
What was discussed?
What was hypothised between these two colossal icons of the 20th Century.
Whatever it was...
...they seemed to be enjoying each other's company.
He with his *"Mad Professor"* wild white long hair was tied up in a ponytail...
...wearing jeans & a black t-shirt...
...didn't care too much for the sun.
...was laying down on they sand, under a rock which provided shade for his very fair skin.

She...
...in her bikini,
...laying on the sand,
...sun baking as one would expect.
...lived for the sun.
...was a child of the sun.

It is almost a scene from a *"Manet"*...
..."Le Soleil Cuit sur la Plage"

"The Don"
06.12.2023

Let Me Entertain You

(Lascia che ti Intrattenere)

Maybe...
...a beer (A Peroni, of course)
...or a proseco, (of course).

Then I could tell you a story...
...about this or that,

...nothing in particular,
...it could range from politics to popular culture (& anything in between).
Then, I'll probably pick up my guitar,
...and strum a few that I know, Am G & F),
...and probably sing you a song (you know the one, I only have one song to sing),
...after I play the first couple of chords, you'll recognise it straight away...
..."All Along the Watchtower".

You can't help yourself but sing along.
..."There must be someway outta here,
Said the Joker to the Thief."

"The Entertainer" has entertained you!

You are happy!

And now to the next person...
..."Let me entertain you!"
Can I offer you a drink?

Maybe...

"The Don"
07.12.2023

My Life as a Wog: Haggling
(La Mia Vita da Wog: Mercanteggiare)

One of the best things that I inherited from my father...
...*probably, the only good thing.*
...*he was a real "arsehole",*
...*he was an old patriarch,*
...*basically, he was a "FASCIST"!*
But I digress...
...*back to the haggling story.*

My father was the BEST haggler there ever was.
He was FANTASTIC.
It was a game to him...
...*and he knew how to play it...*
...*VERY WELL*!

He would haggle over ten cents.
See, you have to understand his thinking...
...to him it was not the money *(even though, of course, it was still very important)*.

You see he a *"certain"* amount in his mind.
He already had a price fixed in his head & he would not budge from it...
...*NO MATTER WHAT*!
That figure was immutable...
...*not negotiable*!

A story that comes to mind *(I must've been about six or seven, back in 1966)* which illustrates this point clearly is my father buying furniture in our local store in Five Dock, called *"Whitford's"*.
This store sold everything...
...*furniture,*
...*electrical appliances,*
...*bedding,*
...*kitchens.*

It was a family business owned by *John Whitford*, who also worked there, selling.

He was a straight up & down old style Aussie.
Very friendly, very fair & very welcoming.
He LOVED the Italians *(and there were lot of Italians in Five Dock at the time)*.
Anyway, I can't remember what we were actually buying but this episode has stuck in my brain ever since.
Negotiating time...
...my father was at his breathtaking best.,
...the dance had started.

John made his first move, stated a price.
My father makes a counter move...
...a bold and some would say even a reckless one.
But if you do...
...you underestimate my father.
His offer $100 less.

John does not look surprised by this bold move...
...and with a genital smile, makes his second move...
...I can take $50 off but the absolute best that I can.
My dad, ponders this for while & then makes his next offer...
..."$75" off.
John, comes over to my father and with a smile, he puts his arm around my dad's should...
..."Joe", he says *"I've got to make a living too!"*
But using the *"moral card"*, was not going to work on my dad *(because he was as immoral as they come)*!
My just to walk away towards the exit door, as if he was leaving.

But I knew he was doing.
Unbeknownst to anyone, he was stealthy pulling out a wad of cash from his pocket, turns around & slowly walking back towards John.
When gets up to him looks at John & says...
..."CASH"!
And hands out his holding the wad of money.
John looks down the money, then at my dad & breaks into smile.
"Just for you Joe!"

The deal is down.
Money is exchanged.
Hands are shaken.
Everyone walks away happy.

And I walk away with the gift of haggling!

"The Don"
08.12.2023

Don't FUCKING Work at All!

(Non Lavorare Affatto, CAZZO!)

That is only true if you are born into a rich family,
Or...
...if you are born into a family that has sold their souls to the Devil!

Unfortunately, the rest of us have to work!

"The Don"
18.12.2023

My Hands

(Le Mie Mani)

My hands are not guitarist's hands.
Long & sledder...
...elegantly plucking notes & effortlessly gliding across the fretboard.

They not pianist's hands.
Long & sledder...
...gently playing the keys & effortlessly gliding across the keyboard.

NO!

My hands are thick, short & stumpy.

They are labourer's hands.
Designed for hard, physical work.
A farmer's hands...
...hands made to till the soil & lift huge rocks.
...not elegant hands but rough and hard.

But...
...they are "Lo❤ER's" hands!

What are your hands like?

"The Don"
21.12.2023

Torn Between Fucks

(Diviso Tra Una Scopata e L'altra)

Give a fuck!
Don't give a fuck!
I'm torn between fucks!

"The Don"
24.12.2023

And the World Took Him to His Grave

(E Il Mondo Lo Portò Nella Sua Tomba)

He *thought*.
He *analysed*.
He *hypothised*.
He *philosophised*.
He *postulated*.
He *pontificated*.
He *argued*.
He *struggled*.
He *fought*.
He *prayed*.
He *LO♥ED*.
He *lived*.
He *died*.
And the World took him to his grave!

He sought *God*.
He sought the *Devil*...
...and everything in-between.
He sought *"The Truth"*!
He sought the *answers of the Universe*.
He sought to *live life...*
...and fight Death.
Finally,
He sought out *solitude*!

And the World took him to his grave!

"The Don"
26.12.2023

Sleeping Isn't Death!

(Dormire Non è la Morte!)

Sleeping isn't Death...
...but it's the closest thing to it that we'll experience whilst we are alive!

"The Don"
28.12.2023

When the Sky Falls Down
(Quando il Cielo Cade)

When the sky falls down...
...keep your eyes open.

Do not *flinch*!
Do not *squint*!
Do not *blink*!
Whatever you do...
...DON'T close your eyes!

Keep your eyes open.
Look up at the sky.
Face it, eye to eye.

Do not *flinch*!
Do not *squint*!
Do not *blink*!
Whatever you do...
...DON'T close your eyes!

When the sky falls down!

"The Don"
29.12.2024

Predator

(Predatore)

I am a predator.
It's like some primal, primitive, primordial instinct.
It pervades my every action.
The instinct to *"predate"*.
The instinct to hunt.
The challenge of the conquest.
The pursuit.
The game.
The thrill.

It oozes out of every pour of my body.
Like a stench emanating from my body.
I can't help it.
I can't control.
It's in my psyche.
It's in my very fibre.
It's in my DNA.
I am a predator!

BEWARE...
...I am on the prowl.
...I am predatious.
...I am a predator.
Watch OUT...
...I'll be coming after you!

"On the prowl,
thats how we get our fun
On the prowl,
now don't you tell my mom
On the prowl,
about the company I keep
On the prowl."

"On the Prowl" - Ol' 55
Songwriters: Jon Cleary/Thomas Fitzpatrick/Edward J Washington

"The Don"
31.12.2023

Self-Control

(Autocontrollo)

I DO have the ability of *"Self-control"*...
...*I just choose NOT to use it!*

"The Don"
03.01.2024

People Can Change
(Le Persone Possono Cambiare)

People CAN change...
...but very few ACTUALLY do!

"The Don"
04.01.2024

Boring

(Noioso)

I'm *boring*.
You are *boring*.
We are all *boring*.
I find people who have supposedly *"interesting"* things to say...
...*BORING*!

They talk about *Aristotle, Descartes, Neitsche, Camus, Sartre and so on...*
...*wank, wank wank!*
BORING!

They are just arrogant!
Saying, *"Look at me! Look at me!"*
They are *"attention seekers"*...
...*BORING*!

I much prefer people who have nothing to say!.
They have no pretences.
They know that that they are boring!
At least they are honest.
I much prefer these type of people.
People who know they a *BORING*!

I LO♥E boring people.
I LO♥E myself.
Because...
...*I am BORING*!

"I'm bored
I'm the chairman of the bored
I'm a lengthy monologue
I'm livin' like a dog

I'm bored".

I bore myself to sleep at night
I bore myself in broad daylight
'Cause I'm bored
Just another slimy bore

I'm free to bore my well-bought friends
And spend my cash until the end
'Cause I'm bored
I'm bored

I'm the chairman of the board

I'm sick
I'm sick of all my kicks
I'm sick of all the stiffs
I'm sick of all the dips
I'm bored

I bore myself to sleep at night
I bore myself in broad daylight
'Cause I'm bored
I'm bored

Just another dirty bore

All right doll-face
Come on and bore me

I'm sick
I'm sick of all my kicks
I'm sick of all the stiffs
I'm sick of all the dips

I'm sick
I'm sick when I go to sleep at night
I'm still sick in the broad daylight
'Cause I'm bored
I'm bored."

"I'm the chairman of the Bored."
Written & perfomed by: Iggy Pop

"The Don"
07.01.2023

None of Us Are Real

(Nessuno di Noi è Reale)

None of us are real...
...we were FOOLS to believe we could be!

"Quote from "Foundation"-S2E10"

"The Don"
08.01.2024

Don't Ask Me for Any Advice
(Non Shiedermi Nessun Consiglio)

Don't ask me for any advice!

I have no FUCKING idea what's going on...
...so don't ask me for any advice.

"The Don"
08.01.2024

Fool's Hope

(La Speranza dello Sciocco)

It's a *"fools"* hope to believe in something that's impossible.

"Ahhhhhhhh!"
"I don't know...
...sometimes it's good to be a FOOL!"

"The Don"
08.01.2024

Alchemy

(Alchimia)

Alchemy...
...the turning of Lead into Gold.

The process of internal transformation...
..."ENLIGHTENMENT"!

"The Don"
09.01 2024

Lonesome Highway

(Autostrada Solitaria)

We are born alone.
We die alone.
An in-between we travel along the *"Lonesome Highway"*.

It is a lonely road.
You travel alone.
No one else can come with you.
No matter how much you try.
No matter how much you want them to.
No matter whoever you prey to.
No one can walk with you.
You walk alone.
You will always walk alone.
As you have always walked alone.
You will forever walk alone...
...on the *"Lonesome Highway"*.

"The Don"
11.01.2024

"Personable" Shit

(Merda "personale")

He's very personable.
But...
...he's full of shit!

"Personable" shit!

"The Don"
12.01.2023

Pissing in the Wind

(Pisciare nel vento)

Pissing in the wind.
I'm just pissing in the wind!

"The Don"
12.01.2024

Control

(Controllo)

Control...
...such a misunderstood concept.
It's not about control over others...
...that give you power.

It is control over oneself.

To control one's...
...emotions.
...thoughts.
...desires.
...pleasures
...wants.
...actions.
...behaviour.

This is what *"real"* control is really all about.

If you can control yourself...
...you can control your existence!

"The Don"
13.01.2024

Charlatan

(Ciarlatano)

He's a *fraud*.
He's a *fake*.
He's an *imposter*.
He's a *poser*.
He's an *opportunist*.
He's a *liar*.
He's a *fabricator*.
He's a *manipulator*.
He's a *schemer*.
He's a *"snake in the grass"*.
He's a *"wolf in sheep's clothing"*.
He's an *appropriator*.
He's a *"misinformer"*.
He's a *pretender*.
He's an *"attention seeker"*.
He's a *narcissist*.
He's a *Capitalist (he has shares in Uranium mining)*!
He's a *chameleon*.
He's a *"Machiavellian"*.
He's a *"bullshit artist"*.
He's a *wanker*.
He's a charlatan.

Whatever you do...
...DON'T TRUST him!

"The Don"
15.01.2024

The Game of Life

(Il Gioco della Vita)

The game of life...
...is rigged.

You cannot win.
You have lost before you begin.
No matter how hard you try...
...you cannot win.

You ALWAYS lose.

No matter what you do.
The *"House"* ALWAYS wins.
The game of life is rigged!

Just letting you know!
If that helps you!

"The Don"
18.01.2024

Out of the NOISE

(Fuori dal RUMORE)

Out of the NOISE...
...comes...
...MUSIC!

"The Don"
20.01.2024

Books written by "The Don"

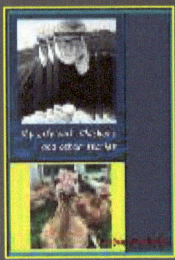

"My Life with Chickens & other stories: I Pity the Poor Immigrant"
Published:
10th September, 2019
Autobiography Book 1:

"Poems for Misfits, Miscreants, Misanthropes, Mavericks, Losers & Malcontents!"
Published:
10th June, 2020
Book of Poems 1

"Poems for Troubled Minds & Trouble Hearts"
Published:
10th August, 2020

Book of Poems 2

"My Life in a CULT & other stories: Everybody Must Get STONED!"
Published:
10th September, 2020
Autobiography Book 2:
15 – 30 years old

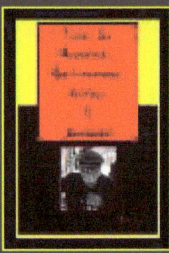

"Poems for Restless Minds & Restless Hearts"
Published:
10th October, 2020
Book of Poems 3

"Poems for Anarchists, Revolutionaries, Outlaws & Dissidents!"
Published:
10th November, 2020

Book of Poems 4

"Poems for Non-Thinkers & Eccentrics"
Published:
10th December, 2020
Book of Poems 5

"The Rantings of a Madman"
Published:
10th January, 2021

Book of Poems 6

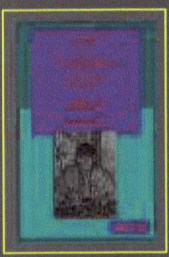

"Poems for Desperate Lovers & Silent Voices"
Published:
10th February, 2021
Book of Poems 7

All available ONLY online

"Poems for Tormented Minds & Tortured Souls"
Published:
10th March, 2021
Book of Poems 8

Books written by "The Don"

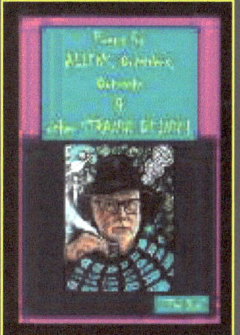

"Poems for ALIENS, Outsiders, Outcasts & other STRANGE BEINGS!"
Published: 10th April, 2021
Book of Poems 9

"Poems for Beings From Another Planet"
Published: 10th May, 2021
Book of Poems 10

"Poems for Mindless Beings & Lost Souls"
Published: 10th June, 2021
Book of Poems 11

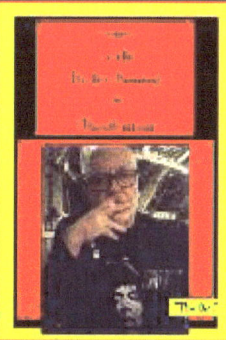

"Poems for the Broken Hearted & Misunderstood
Published: 10th July, 2021
Book of Poems 12

"Poems for Poems for the Bewildered, Dazed & Confused"
10th August, 2021

Book of Poems 13

"Poems for the Outsiders, Displaced, Dispossessed, Discarded & Unwanted"
Published: 10th Sept, 2021
Book of Poems 14

"Poems for Secret Agents, Phantom Agents, Agents of Change, Agent Provocateurs & Agents of Chaos"
Published: 10th Oct, 2021

Book of Poems 15

"Poems for Disenchanted, Disillusioned & Delusional"
Published: 10th November, 2021
Book of Poems 16

All available ONLY online

Books written by "The Don"

"Poems for the Stoners, drugos, ACID takers & Psychedelic LO♥ERS (Everybody Must Get Stoned)"
Published: 10th December, 2021
Book of Poems 17

"Poems for Anarchists, Rebels & Revolutionaries
Published: 10th January, 2022
Book of Poems 18

"Poems for Rebels, Radicals & Revolutionaries (Viva la Révolution!)"
Published: 10th February, 2022
Book of Poems 19

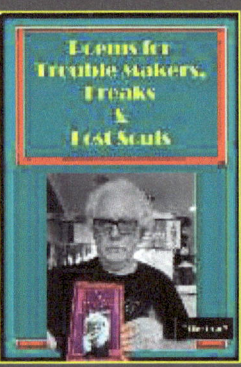

"Poems for Trouble Makers, Freaks & Lost Souls"
Published: 10th March 2022
Book of Poems 20

"Poems for Zombies & the Walking Dead"
Published: 10th April 2022
Book of Poems 21

"Poems for Non-Conformists (Never conform!)"
Published: 10th May 2022
Book of Poems 22

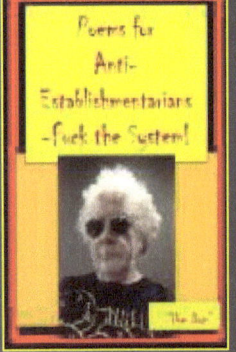

"Poems for Anti-Establishment-arians -Fuck the System!"
Published: 10th June 2022
Book of Poems 23

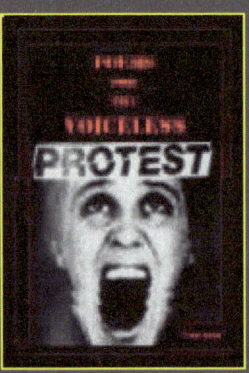

"Poems for the Voiceless"
Published: 10th July 2022
Book of Poems 24

All available ONLY

Books written by "The Don"

"Poems for the Fearless"

Published: 10th August 2022

Book of Poems 25

"Poems for the PEACEMAKER: Make peace NOT war!"
Published: 10th March 2023
Book of Poems 26

Poems for the Forever Young (May you stay forever young!)
Published: 10th June 2023
Book of Poems 27

Poems for the Children of the REVOLUTION!
Published: 5th December 2023

Book of Poems 28

Poems for the L'Innocente!
Published: 10th March 2024
Book of Poems 29

All available ONLY online

Poems for the IMMORTALS (They who die before they die will never die!)
Published: 10th July 2024
Book of Poems 30

Books written by "The Don"

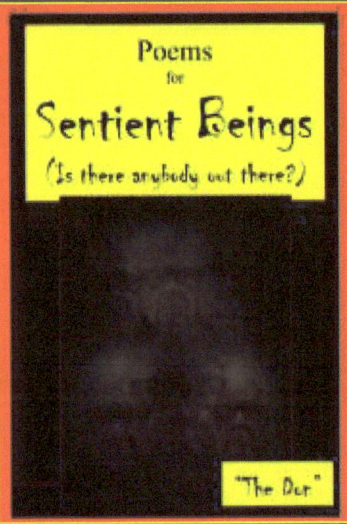

Poems for Sentient Beings (Is there anybody out there?)
Published: 10th December 2024
Book of Poems 31

All available ONLY online

Poems for those Standing on the Edge of Forever
Published: 10th December 2024
Book of Poems 32

Poems for OUTSIDERS!

Published: 10th March 2025

Book of Poems 33

www.ingramcontent.com/pod-product-compliance
Lightning Source LLC
Chambersburg PA
CBHW041724070526
44585CB00006B/140